FILL IN THE GAPS 1

by
Edward R. Rosset

Editorial Stanley

Written by
Edward R. Rosset
Member of the Bachelor of Arts Association
of Euskadi.

Revised by
Beryl Aguado Lait
Principal of Apsley School of English.
Portsmouth - England

Published by
Editorial Stanley

Layout
Angela Gómez Martín

Front page design
Esquema

Apdo. 207 - 20302 IRUN - SPAIN
Telf. (943) 64 04 12 - Fax. (943) 64 38 63

ISBN: 84-7873-276-4
Dep. Leg.: BI- 652-99

First edition 1995
Second edition 1999

Printers
Imprenta RGM

FILL IN THE GAPS 1

Fill in the gaps 1

PAGES	CONTENTS
2-3	TO BE (PRESENT)
4-5	TO HAVE (PRESENT)
6-7	THERE IS - THERE ARE
8-9	SOME - ANY
10-11	WAS - WERE
12-13	SOMEBODY/SOMEONE - ANYBODY/ANYONE - NOBODY/NO-ONE - SOMETHING - ANYTHING - NOTHING
14-15	DO DOES
16-17	POSSESSIVE CASE
18-19	GOING TO
20-21	THERE WAS - THERE WERE
22-23	DID
24-25	FUTURE
26-27	TELL - SAY
28-29	PRESENT PERFECT
30-31	DO - MAKE
32-33	DO - MAKE (cont.)
34-35	CAN - COULD - TO BE ABLE
36-37	AT - IN - ON
38-39	AT - IN - ON (cont.)
40-41	AT - IN - ON (cont.)
42-43	AT - IN - ON (cont.)
44-45	WOULD
46-47	IMPERATIVE
48-49	PASSIVE VOICE
50-51	MUST - HAVE TO
52-53	COMPARATIVES - SUPERLATIVES
54-55	YET - STILL
56-57	DURING - FOR - SINCE - AGO
58-59	QUESTION TAGS
60-61	REPORTED QUESTIONS

Fill in the gaps 1

TO BE (PRESENT)

1. I .... a man and she .... a woman. What .... you?
2. The table .... in the centre of the room and the four chairs .... around the table.
3. 'Good morning. Where .... the boy?' 'The boy John .... with the girl, Susan.'
4. The dog .... with the cat in the garden. They .... playing.
5. The boy .... very tall and the girl .... also very tall. The two .... very tall.
6. 'Peter, ... you in the room?' 'No, I .... not in the room.'
7. 'Where .... the glasses?' 'The glasses .... on the table.
8. 'Where .... the dog?' 'The dog and the cat .... on the chair.'
9. 'Where .... the boys?' The boys .... with the girls in the garden.'
10. 'Where .... the children?' 'Little Susan .... at school and Johnny .... in bed.'
11. The man .... with the woman in the room. They .... sitting on the sofa.
12. 'Mary, ... you a woman?' 'No, I .... not a woman, I .... a girl.'
13. The white table .... in the garden and the chairs .... in the sitting-room.
14. 'Where .... the children?' 'The boys .... with Mr Brown and the girls .... with Mrs Smith.'
15. These children .... very good. They .... very good children.
16. London .... the capital of England. It .... in England.
17. This girl .... small. She .... not a very tall girl.
18. Marian .... a very pretty girl. She .... very pretty.
19. 'Where .... John?, ... he with Mary?' 'Yes, they .... in the sitting-room.'
20. The little girl .... playing with the dog in the garden.

TO BE (PRESENT)

21. Where .... the animals?' 'The two animals .... playing in the park.
22. 'Johnny, ... you a man?' 'No, I .... not a man.' I .... a boy.'
23. 'What .... that on the table?' 'My English book .... on the table.'
24. Where .... John and Peter?' 'They .... in the garden.'
25. 'Where .... London?, ... it in the north?' 'No, it .... in the south.'
26. The policeman .... with the woman. They .... in the street.
27. 'Where .... the chairs?' 'The chairs .... around the table.'
28. The Evans .... in the sitting-room. They .... not in the garden.
29. 'What .... your brother doing?' 'My brother .... playing in the garden.'
30. The man .... sitting on the chair. Where .... the woman sitting?
31. 'Good morning, ... Mr Evans in the house?' 'No, he .... in the garden.'
32. The boys .... in the park. They .... playing football.
33. 'Hello, ... you in the bedroom?' 'No, we .... in the sitting-room.'
34. 'Where .... the cat?' 'The cat and the dog .... with Mrs Smith.'
35. .... the man with the woman?' 'Yes, the man and the woman .... in the garden.'
36. 'Where .... the books?' 'One .... on the chair and two .... on the table.'
37. Jane and Mary .... girls; and John and Peter .... boys.
38. 'Where .... the two women?' 'They .... sitting on the sofa.'
39. The two children .... in the park. They .... playing with the dog.
40. Mr Brown .... not at home. He .... at the bank.

Fill in the gaps 1

TO HAVE (PRESENT)

1. I .... a house. It .... five big rooms.
2. The house .... a nice garden. All the houses .... nice gardens.
3. The children .... a black cat and the woman .... a white dog.
4. She .... a white chair and we .... a black table.
5. They .... four big chairs in the room. We .... only two little chairs.
6. ' .... you a garden?' 'No, we .... not a garden.'
7. The Evans .... not a dog. They .... a cat.
8. ' .... the house four rooms?' 'No; it .... five rooms.'
9. ' .... the Browns a white house?' 'No, they .... not a white house.'
10. ' .... the room a white floor?' 'No, it .... not a white floor.
11. ' .... all these houses gardens?' 'No, these houses .... not gardens.'
12. ' .... the woman a black dog?' 'No; she .... a white cat.'
13. ' .... the boys windows in the room?' 'Yes, they .... two windows.'
14. We .... a white table in the garden near the house.
15. ' .... you a camera?' 'Yes, I .... a very good camera.'
16. In my home town we .... a big supermarket. It .... a big parking area.
17. ' .... you much traffic?' 'Yes, we .... a lot of traffic.'
18. ' .... the door a handle?' 'Yes, all the doors .... handles.'
19. ' .... you a bath in your house?' 'Yes, we .... a bath and a shower.'
20. ' .... the Browns a house in the country?' 'Yes, they ....'

TO HAVE (PRESENT)

21. 'How many brothers .... you got?' 'I .... got two brothers.'

22. '............ you got any sisters?' 'No, I .... got any sisters.'

23. '............ he got a camera?' 'No, he .... got a camera.'

24. It's raining and we .... got an umbrella; .... you got one?'

25. 'How many dogs .... the Browns got?' 'They .... a nice little Terrier.'

26. The Evans .... two TV sets. Little Johnny .... got one in his room.

27. '............ you got a car?' 'No, I .... got a car but my brother .... got one.

28. '............ he got problems?' 'Yes, he ....'

29. We .... got many books in our library, but your library .... got many.

30. That woman .... got a very nice baby. Those women .... also got nice babies.

31. '............ you got a chair in your room?' 'No, I .... got a chair.'

32. My father .... got a very big car. It is very comfortable.

33. 'It's raining, ... you got an umbrella?' 'No; but my brother .... got one.'

34. Our dog is white but he .... got two black legs.

35. The manager .... got many problems, but these people .... got any problems.

36. Our house .... got a red roof. All the houses .... got red roofs.

37. Mr Brown .... got a small shop. All these people .... got small shops.

38. '............ you got a cinema in Croydon?' 'Yes, we .... got a cinema and a theatre.'

39. '............ you got any milk?' 'No, sorry, we .... got any milk.'

40. '............ you got any coffee?' 'No, we .... got coffee, but we .... got some tea.

Fill in the gaps 1

THERE IS · THERE ARE

1. .... a little dog in the park; .... also a big cat.
2. In this house .... eight little rooms and a big kitchen.
3. '.................... a lot of traffic in this street'. 'Yes .... many cars in this town.'
4. In the park .... many dogs, but .... not any cats.
5. .... two lamps on this wall but .... only one lamp on that wall.
6. '.................... any coffee in the cup?' 'No, in the cup .... not any coffee.'
7. '.................... any trees in Richmond Park?' 'Yes, in Richmond Park .... many trees.'
8. '.................... any milk in the fridge?' 'Yes, ... a bottle of milk.'
9. '.................... any people on the beach?' 'Yes, ... many people on the beach.'
10. '.................... a supermarket in this town?' 'Yes, ... two supermarkets.'
11. '.................... many cars on the road.' 'Yes, ... a lot of traffic today.'
12. '.................... many girls in your class?' 'No; .... only one girl in my class.'
13. .... a plane to New York today?' 'Today .... two planes to New York.'
14. '.................... any petrol in the tank?' 'No, ... not any petrol.'
15. '.................... a telephone near here?' 'Well, ... two telephones over there.'
16. '.................... any glasses in the kitchen?' 'In the kitchen .... only one glass.'
17. In this box .... a lot of money; .... many bank notes.
18. '.................... many teachers in your school?' 'Yes, ... fifteen teachers.'
19. .... a lot of noise in this place; .... many people shouting.
20. .... a dog sitting on the grass, and .... two cats standing.

THERE IS · THERE ARE

21. '.......................... a TV set in my room?' 'Well, ... colour televisions in all the rooms.'

22. '.......................... a lot of grass in the garden?' 'No, ... any grass in this garden.'

23. '.......................... many flowers in the garden?' 'Yes, ... a lot of flowers in the garden.'

24. '.......................... any money in the bank?' 'No, in the bank .... any money.'

25. 'How many players .... in a football team?' 'In a football team .... eleven players.'

26. 'How much water .... in the radiator?' 'In the radiator .... very little water.'

27. '.......................... anybody at home?' 'No, ... anybody in the house.'

28. '.......................... many people unemployed?' 'Yes, ... a lot of unemployment.'

29. '.......................... any coffee in the cup?' 'No, in the cup .... any coffee.'

30. '.......................... many houses in this street?' 'No, ... many houses in this street.'

31. '.......................... enough chairs for everybody?' 'No, ... enough chairs for all the guests.'

32. On this beach .... a lot of sand. But on that beach .... any sand.

33. '.......................... a lamp on the wall?' 'Well, ... three lamps on the wall.'

34. '.......................... four rooms in the house?' 'No; .... five rooms.'

35. '.......................... a cat in the garden?' 'No, ... a cat, but .... a dog.'

36. In the English class .... many boys, but .... only one girl.'

37. '.......................... a lot of traffic in this street?' 'Yes, ...'

38. '.......................... six chairs in the garden?' 'No; .... only five.'

39. '.......................... many people at the concert?' 'No, ... many people.'

40. '.......................... any water in the swimming pool?' 'No, ... any water in the swimming pool.'

Fill in the gaps 1

SOME · ANY

1. 'Have you got .... wine?' 'Yes, I have .... wine.'
2. 'Is there .... coffee in the coffee-pot?' 'No, there isn't ....'
3. 'Have we got .... money in the bank?' 'Yes, we have .... but not very much.'
4. 'Is there .... sugar left?' 'No, there isn't .... sugar left.'
5. 'Have you got .... stamps?' 'Yes, I've got .... stamps in my pocket.'
6. 'Are there .... aspirins in the bathroom?'
   'No, there aren't .... ' but I have .... in my pocket.'
7. 'Have you got .... English newspapers?' 'We only have .... American papers.'
8. 'Are there .... English books in the library?' 'There are .... but not many.'
9. 'Have you .... brothers or sisters?' 'I've got two brothers, but I haven't got .... sisters.'
10. 'Has he got .... friends in this town?' 'Yes, he has .... friends.'
11. 'Is there .... wine in the cellar?' 'No; there's only .... beer.'
12. 'Are there .... good hotels in this town?' 'Yes, there are .... very good hotels.'
13. 'Are there .... glasses in the dining-room?' 'No; but there are .... in the kitchen.'
14. 'Have we got .... milk in the house?' 'There are .... bottles in the fridge.'
15. 'Have you got .... trees in your garden?' 'No, we haven't got .... trees.'
16. 'Are there .... chairs in the dining-room?' 'Yes, there are ....'
17. 'Have you got .... money on you?' 'Well, I have ...., but not very much.'
18. 'Is there .... wine in the bottle?' 'No, there isn't ....'
19. 'Are there .... restaurants near the beach?'
    'Yes, there are ....'
20. 'Is there .... coffee left?' 'No, there isn't .... there's only .... tea.'

21. 'Are there .... pubs near the port?' 'Yes, there are ....'

22. In this country there are .... very interesting magazines and newspapers.'

23. 'Are there .... theatres in this town?' 'No, there aren't.............., but there are .... cinemas.'

24. 'Are there .... girls in this school?' 'No, in this school there aren't .... girls.'

25. 'Have you got .... hotels in this village?' 'No; but there are .... a few miles from here.'

26. 'Is there .... sugar in the sugar-bowl?' 'Yes, there is .... '

27. 'Can I have .... more coffee, please?' 'Sorry, we haven't got ....'

28. 'Are there .... books on the table?' 'No, there aren't .... on the table, but there are .... on the chair.

29. 'Are there .... girls playing in the park?' 'No; but there are .... boys playing football.'

30. 'Can you give me .... sugar, please?' 'Sorry, I can't give you ....'

31. 'Have you got .... change?' 'Yes, I have .... in my pocket.'

32. 'Can I have .... tea, please?' 'Sorry, we haven't got .... left.'

33. 'Have you got .... champagne for Christmas?'
'Yes, we have...............'

34. My father only has .... tea for breakfast. He doesn't have .... bread.

35. 'Is there .... grass in the garden?' 'Well, there is .... but not very much.'

36. 'Are there .... wild animals in this zoo?' 'Yes, there are...............'

37. 'Give me .... salt, please!' 'Sorry, we haven't got ....'

38. 'Are there .... supermarkets in this town?' 'There are .... in the centre.'

39. I haven't got .... stamps for this letter. Have you got .... ?

40. 'Are there .... nice villages on the coast?'
'Yes, there are .... along the coast.'

Fill in the gaps 1

WAS · WERE

1. 'Where .... the children yesterday?' 'They .... at the cinema?'
2. 'Where .... your mother?' 'She .... shopping all morning.'
3. '............ you at the concert last night?' 'Yes, I ....'
4. '............ it very cold last winter?' 'Yes, it .... very cold.'
5. 'What .... you reading yesterday?' 'I .... reading a very interesting book.'
6. 'What .... those women doing yesterday?' 'They .... talking.'
7. 'What .... you doing when the teacher came?' 'I .... playing.'
8. 'Last summer we .... in Benidorm. Where .... you?' 'We .... in Scotland.'
9. It .... very cold yesterday morning. It .... not hot.
10. '............ the children good?' 'No, they .... not very good.'
11. You .... watching TV all afternoon. I .... working all day.
12. It .... raining all morning, but it .... not very cold.
13. 'Where .... your brother last night?' 'He .... with me all evening.'
14. Those people .... working all night. They .... on night duty.
15. '............ you good yesterday?' 'Yes, yesterday we .... all very good.'
16. All the pupils .... playing when the teacher came into the classroom.
17. 'Where .... you when I called you?' 'I .... playing in the garden.'
18. My mother .... cooking all morning in the kitchen, and I .... with her.
19. It .... very cold in Europe last winter, but in America it .... very hot.
20. 'Your father .... not very tall when he .... young. He .... short.

21. 'Where .... you on Sunday?' 'On Sunday I .... playing football in the morning.'

22. 'Where .... Daddy yesterday afternoon?' 'He .... in his office until four.'

23. 'Where .... Mr. Evans?' 'He .... visiting a client in Scotland.'

24. 'What .... you doing on Sunday morning in London?' 'I .... visiting a friend.'

25. '.......... Diana at home?' 'Yes, she .... with her mother.'

26. 'What time .... it when your brother came?' 'It .... nine o'clock.'

27. Where .... your mother yesterday?' 'She .... visiting my grandmother.'

28. '.......... you at home yesterday afternoon?' 'Yes, I .... with my brother in the house all day.'

29. 'Those children .... making a lot of noise all morning.'

30. '.......... the tea hot?' 'No, it .... hot; it .... cold.'

31. '.......... the concert good last night?' 'No, it .... very good.'

32. The children .... studying in their bedroom when you came.'

33. '.......... you good at Maths when you .... little, Dad?' 'Yes, I .... very good.'

34. 'Where .... grandfather during the war?' 'He .... on the Russian front.'

35. 'Where .... Mrs. Smith when she had the baby?' 'She .... at the Maternity Hospital in Hackney.'

36. These nurses .... working all night at the hospital.'

37. '.......... the sandwich good?' 'Yes, the two sandwiches .... very good.'

38. '.......... she tired yesterday?' 'Yes, she .... very tired last night.'

39. '.......... it hot on the Costa Brava last summer?' 'Yes, it .... very hot.'

40. '.......... the tea hot?' 'Yes, it .... quite hot, thank you.'

Fill in the gaps 1

SOMEBODY/SOMEONE · ANYBODY/ANYONE · NOBODY/ NO-ONE SOMETHING - ANYTHING - NOTHING

1. 'There is .... in the river. Can you see it?' 'No, I can't see ....'
2. I can see .... yellow near the bank. I think it is a ball.
3. 'Does ..../........... want a ball?' 'No, .../........... wants a ball.
4. 'Are you going to do .... this afternoon?' 'No, I'm not going to do ....'
5. We are going to do .... but I don't know what.'
6. 'Can ..../........... go to that party?' 'Yes, of course, .../........... can come.'
7. 'What have you got in your hand?' 'I haven't got .... in my hand.'
8. 'Can ..../........... tell me what's happening?' 'No, .../........... can tell you what's happening.'
9. ..../........... knows .... in this house.
10. 'Is there .... I can bring you from London?' 'No, I don't want ....'
11. 'Is there .... in that envelope?' 'No, there is .... inside it.'
12. There is ..../........... in that room, and he has .... in his hands.
13. 'I'd like to eat ....' 'No, you can't eat ....'
14. 'Is there .... important in this book?' 'No, there is .... important.'
15. 'Is there .... interesting on at the cinema?' 'Yes, there is .... very interesting.'
16. 'Can ..../........... tell me the title of the film?' 'No, ... can tell you.'
17. 'Has ..../........... got a dictionary?' 'No, ... has a dictionary.'
18. 'Has the prisoner said .... yet?' 'No, he hasn't said .... yet.'
19. 'I will give you .... you want. Just tell me what you want.'
20. 'Has ..../........... seen Robert?' 'No, .../........... has seen him.'

SOMEBODY/SOMEONE · ANYBODY/ANYONE · NOBODY/NO-ONE SOMETHING - ANYTHING - NOTHING

21. ______/______ knows the answer to that question. It's very difficult.
22. ______/______ can learn to play the piano with this method. It's very easy.
23. 'I've got ______ in my eye. Can you see it?' 'Yes, I can see ______.'
24. That little girl doesn't want to eat ______.
25. 'Does ______/______ want ______?' 'No, ______/______ wants ______.'
26. 'There is ______ in that tree. Can you see it?' 'Yes, I can see ______ dark.'
27. 'Does ______/______ want more cake?'
'No, ______/______ wants any more.'
28. 'Does ______/______ want to come with me?'
'No, ______/______ wants to go with you.'
29. 'What is happening over there?' 'Well, ______/______ has fallen into the river.'
30. 'Is there ______ in the box?' 'No, there is ______ inside it.'
31. 'Is there ______ written on that wall?' 'No, there is ______ written on this wall.'
32. 'Is there ______/______ with you?' 'No, there is ______/______ with me.'
33. 'Do you have ______ important to do today?' 'Yes, I have ______ very important to do this morning.'
34. The person coming this afternoon is ______/______ very important, but ______/______ knows his name.
35. 'Can you see ______/______ coming?' 'No, I can't see ______/______ coming this way.'
36. 'Is there ______ important you want to tell me?' 'No, there is ______ important.'
37. 'Is there ______ to eat in the fridge?' 'Yes, there is ______.'
38. 'Does ______/______ want to volunteer for the job?' 'No, ______/______ wants to volunteer.'
39. If you help me with this, I will give you ______ you want.
40. 'Is there ______ we can do this afternoon?' 'No, there is ______.'

Fill in the gaps 1

DO DOES (AUXILIARY VERB)

1. 'When .... your mother do the housework?' 'She does it in the morning.'
2. 'Peter, ... you like watching TV in the mornings?' 'No, I .... like watching TV in the mornings.'
3. 'What .... you do in the evenings?' 'In the evenings I .... do anything.'
4. My brother .... work in the mornings. He only works in the afternoons.
5. 'When .... you do the washing?' 'I do the washing in the afternoon.'
6. '............ your father go to work on Saturdays?' 'No, he .... work on Saturdays.'
7. 'What language .... you speak in the English class?' 'We always speak in English.'
8. '............ you like reading adventure books?' 'No, I .... like reading adventure books.'
9. '............ she buy bread every day?' 'No, she .... buy bread every day.'
10. '............ the children watch a lot of TV at the weekend?' 'No, they .... watch a lot of TV.'
11. 'At what time .... you prepare the tea?' 'I .... prepare the tea until five.'
12. '............ you always speak in English in the English class?' 'No, we .... always speak in English.'
13. 'At what time .... those children finish in the evening?' 'They .... finish until six.'
14. '............ your father take you to the station when it is raining?' 'No, he ....'
15. At what time .... your grandmother go to the supermarket?'
16. 'At what time .... these little girls go to sleep in the evenings?' 'They .... go until nine.'
17. 'What .... you have with your meals? .... you have water?'
18. 'What .... your father do on Sunday mornings?' 'He .... do anything.'
19. 'At what time .... you have lunch on weekdays?' 'We .... have lunch until one.'
20. '............ your children read very much at the weekend?' 'No, they .... read anything.'

DO DOES (AUXILIARY VERB)

21. 'At what time .... you get up on Sundays?' 'I .... get up until midday.'

22. 'In which school .... you study? .... you have lunch at school?' 'No, I .... have lunch at school.'

23. '............ you like your teachers?' 'Well I .... like all of them.'

24. '............ you go to school by bus?' 'No, we .... go by bus; we go on foot.'

25. 'Where .... your brothers and sisters study?' 'They .... study in my school; they go to another school.'

26. 'What .... your mother do?' 'She works at home; she .... go out to work.'

27. 'What .... your mother do with your little sister?' 'She takes her to the nursery.'

28. 'What .... you do on Saturday mornings?' 'I go to school, but I .... go to study.'

29. '............ you play football with your friends?' 'No, they .... like playing football.'

30. '............ it rain much in your country?' 'No, it ....'

31. '............ you like the programmes on TV?' 'No, I .... like them very much.'

32. '............ your father come home for lunch?' 'No, he .... come home for lunch.'

33. 'Where .... he have lunch?' 'He has lunch near his office.'

34. 'What .... your parents do on Sundays?' 'They stay at home; they .... go out.'

35. '............ you like romantic films?' 'No, I .... like romantic films.'

36. 'Where .... your friend, Peter, live?' 'He lives in Croydon.'

37. I .... like people who shout all the time.

38. .... he want a cup of tea? No, but I ....

39. 'At what time .... you stop for lunch?'

40. '............ children like going to school?' 'No, they .... like going to school.'

Fill in the gaps 1

POSSESSIVE CASE

1. This car belongs to Peter. It is ....
2. The car parked outside my house belongs to my father. It is ....
3. The bicycle leaning against the wall belongs to my brother. It is ....
4. There is a doll on the table in the garden. It belongs to my sister. It is ....
5. That yellow house belongs to our neighbour. It is ....
6. At the door of the house there is a woman. She is the wife of Mr. Robinson. She is ....
7. The boy and the girl in the garden are the children of Mr. and Mrs. Robinson. They are ....
8. The Robinsons have a shop where they sell groceries. They have a ....
9. That little girl is the daughter of Mrs Green. She is ....
10. That young woman is Mary, the niece of the Browns. She is the ....
11. 'What do you know about the father of that girl?' 'I don't know anything about ....'
12. That boy waving is James, the boyfriend of Diana. He is ....
13. 'James is a friend of the cousin of Mary.' 'Yes, I know he is a friend of ....'
14. 'Peter very often plays with the bicycle of John.' 'Yes, I know he plays with ....'
15. 'All these are the toys of the children.' 'Yes, they are ....'
16. 'This is the room of the boys and that is the room of the girls.' 'So this is .... and that is ....!'
17. This is the advice of my father. It is ....
18. That building over there is the school of my sons. It is ....
19. 'The legs of our little dog are white.' 'So .... are white!'
20. 'Is that the bicycle of your daughter?' 'Yes, it is ....'

21. My mother is buying meat at ....'

22. We need fish for dinner. I'll go to buy some at ....'

23. 'The storm we had last week caused a lot of damage.' 'Yes, I know that .... caused a lot of damage.'

24. 'Have you got a holiday?' 'Yes, I've got two weeks. I've got ....'

25. 'Tomorrow is the anniversary of my parents.' 'Is it really ....?'

26. 'The dog of Mr. Carter is barking in the garden.' 'Yes, ... is barking in the garden.'

27. 'The meeting of tomorrow has been cancelled.' 'Yes, I know that .... has been cancelled.'

28. 'Those are the children of the King of Nepal.' 'So, those are the ....?'

29. These are the bicycles of those boys. They are ....'

30. 'The tails of those two dogs are black.' 'Yes, ... are black.'

31. 'I think I heard the voice of a child.' 'Yes, it was a ....'

32. 'The job that Jimmy is doing is the job of a man.' 'Yes, it is a ....'

33. 'Is that the book of your brother on the table?' 'Yes, it is ....'

34. 'Is *D. Quixote* the best work of Cervantes?' 'Yes, *D. Quixote* is ....'

35. 'Is that the mother of John, Mike and Peter?' 'Yes, she is ....'

36. 'This is better than the one Peter has.' 'Yes, it is better than ....'

37. 'That is the same as the one my mother has.' 'Yes, it is the same as ....'

38. 'The exports of Great Britain have fallen lately.' 'Yes, ... have fallen lately.'

39. 'Why don't you follow the advice of people?' 'I don't like following ....'

40. To get to the lake we have a walk of two hours. We have .... to get to the lake.

Fill in the gaps 1

GOING TO

1. Today we .... to have lunch very late.
2. At what time .... your brothers .... to come tonight?
3. I .... to make some coffee. Do you want some, Robert?
4. What .... mother .... to make for dinner next Sunday?
5. '.......... you .... on holiday this year?' 'Yes, we are going in July?'
6. 'When .... you .... to post the letter?' 'I .... not .... to post it today.'
7. '.......... you .... to fry the fish?' 'Yes, I .... to fry it now.'
8. 'When .... you .... to buy a new car.' 'I .... not .... to buy a new car.'
9. ' At what time .... the children .... to come?' 'They .... to come very late?'
10. '.......... Jennifer .... to play in your team?' 'No, she .... not .... to play with us.'
11. Mum, what .... you .... to prepare for lunch today?
12. '.......... you .... by train?' 'No, we .... by plane.'
13. 'Mrs Evans .... to paint her kitchen green. What colour .... you .... to paint yours?
14. 'When .... the Evans .... to come to see us?' 'They .... not .... to come.'
15. 'When .... you .... to publish your new book?' 'I .... to publish it this year.'
16. '.......... you .... to do the shopping today, Mum?' 'Yes, I .... to the supermarket in a few minutes.'
17. '.......... the children .... to catch the school bus?' 'No, they .... not .... to catch it.'
18. 'When .... you .... to type these letters?' 'I .... to type them this afternoon.'
19. 'What explanation .... you .... to give to your teacher?' 'I .... not .... to give him any explanation.'
20. '.......... the little boy .... to drink the milk?' 'No, he .... not .... to drink it.'

21. 'What .... your friends .... to do next Sunday?'
'They .... for a picnic.'

22. I think that my girlfriend .... to buy me a present for my birthday.

23. Look at those clouds. I think that today it .... to rain.

24. 'Mum, I .... to climb that tree.' 'Be careful. You .... to fall.'

25. 'What .... the Government .... to do about unemployment?'

26. 'Where .... you .... to hang that picture?' 'I .... to hang it in the hall.'

27. '............ you .... to listen to the news on the radio?' 'No, I .... to watch it on TV.'

28 'Be careful with that jar. You .... to break it.'

29. 'When .... you .... to sell the house?' 'We .... not .... to sell it.'

30. '............ your daugther .... to get married?' 'No, she .... not .... to get married.'

31. '............ you .... to buy drinks for the party?' 'Yes, I .... to buy some.'

32. 'What colour .... you .... to paint the room?' 'We .... to paint it blue.'

33. '............ the Smiths .... on holiday this year?' 'No, they .... not ....'

34. '............ you .... to pass your exams?' 'Yes, I .... to pass all my exams.'

35. '............ you .... to come for dinner tonight?' 'No, I .... not .... to come tonight.'

36. '............ Mum .... to make tea?' 'No, she .... not .... to make tea. She .... to make coffee.'

37. 'I .... to buy some sweets. Do you want some?' 'No, I .... not .... to eat any sweets today.'

38. 'Where .... you .... to take the children this summer?'
'We .... to take them to the country.

39. 'We .... to have an exam this afternoon.' '............ you .... to pass it?'

40. 'My boyfriend told me that he .... to give me a surprise.' 'What surprise

Fill in the gaps 1

THERE WAS · THERE WERE

1. ' ______ many people at the concert last night?'
'No, ______ not many people.'
2. ' ______ a lot of noise last night?' 'No, ______ very little noise.'
3. ' ______ many cars on the roads yesterday?'
'Yes, ______ many cars.'
4. ' ______ a lot of traffic last Sunday?' 'Yes, ______ a lot of traffic.'
5. In the old days ______ twenty shillings in a pound.
6. ' ______ any whisky in the bottle last night?'
'Well, ______ not very much.'
7. ' ______ any football matches last week?'
'Well, ______ one.'
8. ' ______ any milk for breakfast on Sunday?'
'No, ______ not any milk.'
9. ' ______ a full moon last night?'
'Yes, ______ a full moon.'
10. ' ______ any tickets yesterday for next Saturday's concert?'
'Yes,' ______ many.'
11. ' ______ any water in the fridge yesterday?' 'Yes,' ______ two bottles of water.'
12. ' ______ any flights to New York last Sunday?' 'No, ______ no flights to New York last Sunday.'
13. ' ______ many people waiting to get into the cinema.
14. 'What' ______ on the hall table last night?' ' ______ several letters.'
15. ' ______ many people in England last century?'
'No,' ______ not many.'
16. ' ______ a good film on TV last night?' 'No,' ______ not a film on TV.'
17. When I was a child' ______ many trees in that park.
18. ' ______ a long queue of hungry people waiting to get something to eat.
19. ' ______ any oxygen left in the aqua-lung?' 'No, ' ______ not any oxygen left in the bottles.'
20. ' ______ any water in the radiator yesterday?' 'No, ______ not any water.'

THERE WAS · THERE WERE

21. 'Do you know if there is money in the bank?' 'Well, yesterday .... any money.'

22. 'How many people .... on Saturday at the concert?' 'Well, ... very few people.'

23. '.................................. many hotels in this town when you were a child?' 'No, ... many.'

24. '.................................. many TV sets in the 60's?' 'No, ... many TV sets.'

25. '.................................. much time for playing in your young days?' 'No, ... much time for playing.'

26. '.................................. many wars in the old days?' 'Yes, ... many wars.'

27. '.................................. any coffee in the coffee-pot this morning?' 'No, ...'

28. '.................................. any good programmes last night on TV?' 'No, ... any good programmes.'

29. '.................................. any clean cups in the kitchen this morning?' 'No, ... any.'

30. '.................................. any Chinese restaurants in this town years ago?' 'Well, ... one.'

31. 'How many trees .... in this street before they cut them down?' '.................................. twenty.'

32. 'How much milk .... in the fridge last night?' Well, ... three bottles.'

33. 'How many children .... in your school when you were a child?' '.................................. about four hundred.'

34. 'How many wonders .... in ancient times?' '.................................. seven.'

35. 'How much beer .... in the barrel yesterday?' '.................................. any beer. .... It was empty.'

36. 'How many elephants .... in Hannibal's army?' 'I think .... about thirty.'

37. '.................................. any petrol in the tank when you took the car this morning?' 'No, ... any petrol in the tank.'

38. '.................................. many tourists in Benidorm in August?' 'Yes, ... a lot of tourists.'

39. '.................................. many people at the hypermarket last Saturday?' 'Yes, ... lots of people.'

40. '.................................. anything to do in the evenings in your young days?'

Fill in the gaps 1

DID (AUXILIARY VERB)

1. 'At what time .... you .... to bed on Christmas eve?' 'I went to bed at 2 a.m.' (go)
2. 'What .... you .... to do last night?' 'I .... to do anything.' (want)
3. ' .... you .... to the cinema with Mary?' 'No, I .... with Mary, I went with Lucy.' (go)
4. ' .... the baby .... during the night?' 'No, it .... during the night.' (cry)
5. 'At what time .... you .... dinner last night?' 'I had dinner at eight.' (have)
6. ' .... you .... the night in London?' 'No, I .... the night in London.' (spend)
7. ' .... you .... what you wanted to do?' 'No, I .... what I wanted to do.' (do)
8. 'At what time .... he .... home?' 'He arrived home very late.' (arrive)
9. When .... your father .... this book?' 'He .... this book until last year.' (write)
10. 'Why .... you .... the tennis match?' 'I lost it because I couldn't concentrate.' (lose)
11. .... the children .... the vase?' 'No, they .... it.' (break)
12. Mary, ... you .... on Saturday night?' 'No, we .... ' (go out)
13. 'Johnny, ... you .... a shower?' 'No, I .... a shower. I had a bath.' (have)
14. 'Where .... your friend .... that book?' 'He bought it at the bookshop in High Street.' (buy)
15. 'When .... your mother .... the shopping yesterday?' 'She .... the shopping yesterday.' (do)
16. 'Why .... you .... late?' 'Because the train arrived late.' (come)
17. 'At what time .... the children .... to bed?' 'They .... to bed until eleven.' (go)
18. 'Mr. Brown, ... you .... much when you were young?' 'No, I .... very much.' (smoke)
19. 'When .... you .... playing tennis, Arantxa?' 'I started at the age of ten.' (start)
20. ' .... you .... your friend at the station?' 'No, I .... him.' (meet)

21. 'Why ______ you ______ at the red light?' 'Because I ______ it.' (stop) (see)

22. 'Why ______ you ______ for me?' 'Because it was late.' (wait)

23. 'Why ______ you ______ last night?' 'Because I was tired.' (go out)

24. 'Why ______ you ______ to play cards last Saturday?' 'Because I ______ time.' (come) (have)

25. ' ______ you ______ at Oxford?' 'No, I ______ at Oxford. I studied at Cambridge.' (study)

26. ' ______ Diana ______ a baby?' 'Yes, she had a fine baby last Saturday.' (have)

27. 'What hotel ______ you ______ at?' 'I ______ at any hotel.' (stay)

28. 'What ______ you ______ for breakfast?' 'I ______ any breakfast.' (have)

29. ' ______ it ______ much last winter?' 'No, it ______ much.' (rain)

30. 'Why ______ your brother ______ the letter?' 'Because he ______ time.' (write) (have)

31. ' ______ you ______ the film?' 'No, I ______ it.' (like)

32. ' ______ you ______ Mr. Brian in London?' 'No, I ______ him.' (meet)

33. ' ______ you ______ me the truth?' 'Yes, I told you the truth.' (tell)

34. ' ______ the children ______ a good time at the party?' 'Yes, they had a very good time.' (have)

35. 'Where ______ you ______ your summer holidays?' 'Well, we ______ anywhere. We stayed at home.' (spend) (go)

36. 'Why ______ Julie ______ to school yesterday?' 'Because she was ill.' (go)

37. 'When ______ you ______ to him?' 'I spoke to him last Sunday?' (speak)

38. 'Jimmy, ______ you ______ all the medicine?' 'No, I ______ all the medicine.' (take)

39. ' ______ you ______ Frank and Elsa in London?' 'No, I ______ them in London.' (see)

40. 'Where ______ she ______ to sing so beautifully?' 'She went to singing classes.' (learn)

Fill in the gaps 1

FUTURE (SHALL - WILL)

1. 'When .... you .... the new car?'
'I .... probably .... it next month.' (buy)
2. 'When .... you .... my bicycle, Daddy?' 'I .... it tonight.' (repair)
3. 'At what time .... the train .... tomorrow?' 'The train .... at five.' (leave)
4. 'My friend .... not .... on this trip because he hasn't got any money.' (go)
5. Are you cold Madam? .... I .... the window for you?' (close)
6. It's very hot today. .... we .... to the beach, boys?' (go)
7. I'm sure that you .... your exam if you study hard.' (pass)
8. 'At what time .... you .... tonight?'
'I .... at eleven.' (come)
9. ' .... I .... the suitcase for you, Katty?'
'Yes, please. I .... very grateful.' (carry) (be)
10. ' .... the little child .... well?' 'Yes, he .... well soon.' (get)
11. ' .... we .... to the disco tonight, Jenny?' 'Yes, I .... very happy to go.' (go) (be)
12. ' .... it .... tonight?' 'Yes, it .... probably ....' (rain)
13. ' .... we .... to the cinema tomorrow?'
'Yes, it's a good idea.' (go)
14. ' .... you .... me the newspaper when you go out?' 'OK, I .... it for you.' (buy)
15. If it doesn't rain tomorrow we .... for a picnic in the country. (go)
16. If I am lucky tomorrow I .... the lottery.' (win)
17. 'At what time .... you .... tonight?' 'I think I .... at eight o'clock.' (finish)
18. ' .... you .... all the milk?' 'No, I .... not .... it.' (drink)
19. ' .... Mr. Brown .... to London next week?' 'No, he .... not ....' (go)
20. ' .... the children .... early tonight?' 'No, they .... not .... early.' (finish)

FUTURE (SHALL - WILL)

21. ' ______ you ______ tennis tomorrow?' 'No, we ______ tennis.' (play)
22. ' ______ your father ______ to the teacher?' 'Yes, he ______ to him.' (speak)
23. 'Jimmy, ______ you ______ all the potatoes?' 'No, I ______ them.' (eat)
24. 'When ______ your father ______ home?' 'He ______ tomorrow night.' (come)
25. ' ______ we ______ Jerry in hospital?' 'Yes, let's visit him.' (visit)
26. 'Mr. Brian, ______ you ______ a whisky?' 'No, I ______ anything today, thank you.' (have)
27. ' ______ I ______ the letter for you, Dad?' 'Yes, please.' (post)
28. ' ______ it ______ cold tonight?' 'No, it ______ very cold.' (be)
29. ' ______ you ______ him?' 'Yes, I ______ him tomorrow.' (pay)
30. ' ______ your son ______ in America next year?' 'Yes, he ______ in Los Angeles.' (study)
31. ' ______ you ______ operated on soon?' 'I ______ operated on until next month.' (be)
32. ' ______ we ______ for a drink, boys?' 'Yes, let's go out.' (go out)
33. Next year we ______ our holidays in Greece, it's too hot in there. We ______ them in Spain. (spend)
34. 'What ______ you ______, John?' 'I ______ a whisky and soda.' (have)
35. ' ______ you ______ tennis with me tomorrow?' 'No, I ______ with you.' (play)
36. ' ______ you ______ the restaurant bill?' 'OK, I ______ the bill.' (pay)
37. 'What time ______ I ______ tonight, Mum?' 'Come before nine.' (come)
38. ' ______ we ______ a party tonight, boys?' 'Yes, let's have a party.' (have)
39. ' ______ you ______ a letter to your uncle, Jim?' 'Yes, I ______ it tonight.' (write)
40. ' ______ you ______ to Daddy, Mum?' 'OK, I ______ to him tonight.' (speak)

Fill in the gaps 1

TELL · SAY

1. 'What did your brother .... last night?' 'He didn't .... anything.'
2. 'What did your sister .... you?' 'She didn't .... me anything.'
3. 'What did you ....?' 'I didn't .... anything.'
4. 'What did you .... your mother?' 'I .... her the truth.'
5. 'Mum, ... us a story.' 'OK, I will .... you a nice story.'
6. 'Dad, ... me what happened.' 'OK, I'll .... you what happened.'
7. 'What did your father ....?' 'He .... that he will come tomorrow.'
8. 'What did your father .... you?' 'He .... me that he will come tomorrow.'
9. Your brother .... me a lie. He is always .... lies.'
10. My grandmother liked to .... fairy stories. She was always .... us stories.'
11. 'I'm going to .... you what happened last night.'
12. 'Will you .... us what is going to happen?' 'I will .... you tomorrow.'
13. 'Did she .... when they are going to get married?' 'No, she didn't ....'
14. 'What did you .... the children?' 'I didn't .... them anything.'
15. 'What did Mum ....?' 'She .... that they are coming back tomorrow.'
16. 'Did he .... the truth at the trial?' 'Yes, I think he .... the truth.'
17. 'You mustn't .... lies. You must always .... the truth.'
18. 'She .... that she had heard the news on the radio.' 'She .... me about the accident.'
19. 'Come here', he .... He .... the girl to go there.
20. 'What did the girls .... you?' 'They .... that they'll be coming back late.'

21. 'Did he ______ anything?' 'Well, he didn't ______ his mother anything.'

22. 'I'm going to ______ all those people to go home.' 'OK, ______ them.'

23. Mr. and Mrs Brown ______ their children not to make so much noise. They ______ them to keep quiet.

24. 'What did you ______ last night. I didn't understand you.' 'I ______ that I'll do it.'

25. 'Who did you ______ took you to the cinema?' 'I didn't ______ anything.'

26. 'What did your cousin ______ you about the new job?' 'He ______ that he's got it.'

27. 'What are you going to ______ your father about it?' 'I'll ______ him the truth.'

28. 'What did they ______ about the weather?' 'They ______ that it's going to be fine.'

29. Yesterday they ______ that it's was going to rain. And now they are ______ that it's going to be fine.

30. ' ______ me what you are going to do this afternoon.' 'OK, I'll ______ you in a minute.'

31. Don't ______ lies. Little children mustn't ______ lies.'

32. My children always ______ the truth. They never ______ lies.

33. 'What did your brother ______ when he came last night?' 'He didn't ______ anything.'

34. 'What did Dad ______ those people?' 'He ______ them to come back some other time.'

35. 'Did your sister ______ anything about her new boyfriend?' 'She ______ that he is very nice.'

36. 'Are you going to ______ anything else?' 'No, I'm not going to ______ anything else.

37. John, will you please ______ your sister to wash her hands!

38. 'Is she pretty?' 'They ______ that she is pretty and intelligent.'

39. 'What did the teacher ______?' 'He ______ that we musnt' leave without ______ him.'

40. They ______ in the garage that they have already ______ you about the

Fill in the gaps 1

PRESENT PERFECT

1. '.................... you .... reading the book?' 'No, I .... yet.' (finish)
2. '.................... the children .... their homework?' 'No, they .... it yet.' (do)
3. 'Peter, ... you .... the medicine?' 'No, I .... it yet.' (take)
4. '.................... your father .... yet?' 'Yes, he .... already ....' (phone)
5. '.................... the children .... the window pane?' 'Yes, they .... it.' (break)
6. 'How many books .... you ....?' 'I .... six books.' (write)
7. '.................... you ever .... caviar?' 'No, I .... never .... caviar.' (eat)
8. '.................... they ever .... to the USA?' 'No, they .... never .... to the USA.' (be)
9. 'Is this the first time that you .... a car?' 'Yes, this is the first time that I .... a car.' (drive)
10. '.................... you .... on holiday recently?' 'No, I .... a holiday for a long time.' (be) (take)
11. '.................... you .... the letters?' 'Yes, I .... just .... them.' (post)
12. 'How many times .... you .... in love?' 'I .... never .... in love. (fall)
13. '.................... you .... Jimmy lately?' 'No, I .... him for a month.' (see)
14. '.................... you .... to your parents?' 'I .... already .... to them three times this month.' (write)
15. '.................... you .... Shakespeare?' 'No, I .... never .... Shakespeare.' (read)
16. 'How long .... you .... living in this house?' 'I .... in this house for 20 years.' (be) (live)
17. 'How many marathons .... he ....?' 'He .... three marathons.' (run)
18. '.................... you .... Mr. Clinton?' 'Yes, I .... already .... him.' (meet)
19. '.................... you .... in this business for a long time?' 'No, I .... in this business very long.' (be)
20. 'What .... you .... doing this morning?' 'I .... reading.' (be)

PRESENT PERFECT

21. '__________ the thieves __________ any money?' 'Yes, they __________ a lot of money from the bank.' (steal)

22. '__________ you already __________ the telegram?' 'No, I __________ it yet.' (send)

23. '__________ the children __________ good this morning?' 'Yes, they __________ very good.' (be)

24. Look at the clouds! It __________ raining since last Wednesday.' (be)

25. These children __________ playing all morning.' (be)

26. Those two men __________ taking photographs of the building.' (be)

27. 'How long __________ you __________ studying English for?' 'I __________ studying English for five years.' (be)

28. 'Does it rain much in this country?' 'In this country it __________ for years.' (rain)

29. 'Mary, __________ you __________ your mother?' 'No, I __________ her this morning.' (see)

30. Mum, I __________ the photos yet. __________ you __________ them from the shop?' (see) (collect)

31. 'It's a very nice film. __________ you __________ it?' 'No, I __________ it yet.' (see)

32. He __________ several races this year. __________ you __________ any?' (win)

33. I __________ twenty letters this morning. How many __________ you __________ ?' (type)

34. He __________ five photographs. How many __________ you __________ ?' (take)

35. I __________ always __________ getting up early in the morning.' (like)

36. That girl __________ always __________ very lazy. She __________ never __________ very industrious.' (be)

37. 'Johnny, __________ you __________ all the meat?' 'No, I __________ it all.' (eat)

38. They __________ a match since October. They __________ all their matches.' (win) (lose)

39. He __________ already __________ five film stars. (marry)

40. 'I __________ three umbrellas this winter. __________ you ever __________ anything?' (lose)

Fill in the gaps 1

DO · MAKE

1. 'What will you ____________ during your summer holidays?' 'Well, I'll probably ____________ nothing.
2. 'What are these people ________?' 'I think they are ________ a hole in the road.'
3. 'Is there anything to ____________ in this village?' 'No, there's nothing much to ____________ unless you ____________ some friends.'
4. 'My daughter loves ____________ the housework. She likes ____________ the beds, dusting the furniture, etc.'
5. 'Are you going to ____________ all the exercises today?' 'Yes, I am ____________ a lot of progress.'
6. 'The Minister ____________ a good speech last night.' 'Yes, at last, they have ____________ something about the problem.'
7. 'How many mistakes did you ____________ in the dictation yesterday?' 'I ____________ seven mistakes.'
8. 'Will you ____________ me a favour?' 'Yes, what can I ____________ for you?'
9. 'Children, do you ____________ your own beds?' 'Yes, we ____________ them every day.'
10. 'Jimmy, you are not ____________ very much work. You must ____________ more work at home.'
11. Look at those people. They are going to ____________ a fire in the woods!
12. You've ____________ it all wrong. You have to ____________ it again.
13. That old man ____________ a lot of money after World War II. He ____________ a fortune.
14. I am sure that we are going to ____________ very good business in this country.
15. Peter, ________ an effort, will you! Go to your room and ________ some work.
16. 'Is it difficult to ____________ a Spanish omelette?' 'Well, if you ____________ things properly it's not difficult to ____________ it.'
17. 'Hello, boys. Have you ____________ the written exercises?' 'Yes, sir. We have already ____________ them.'
18. Those boys over there are not ____________ any progress in their studies.
19. My mother is going to have her hair ____________ this afternoon. She has ____________ an appointment at the hairdresser's.
20. Darling, when are the children going to ____________ their homework?

21. This is the girl who usually ____________ the tea in the office. She ____________ it at about four o'clock.

22. My mother always ____________ the shopping in the morning. In the afternoon she doesn't ____________ anything.

23. 'Are you going to ____________ your bed today, Tony?' 'Well, I'll ____________ it this afternoon.'

24. 'Have you ____________ the ironing yet, Mum?' 'No, Susan, I haven't ____________ it yet. I'll ____________ it in a minute.'

25. 'How often do you ____________ this journey, Dad?' 'Well I ____________ this journey when I have business to ____________ in London.'

26. This man says that he is going to ____________ a lot of money ____________ business with you.

27. Boys, we've got to ____________ a plan for next Saturday night. What shall we ____________?'

28. I'll ____________ you a nice cup of tea and you will feel much better, my dear.

29. We will have to ____________ a hole in the garden if we want to plant this tree. Can you ____________ that for me, please?

30. My grandfather was always ____________ complaints. He was always complaining about everything.

31. Good profits are always ____________ in this kind of business.

32. We have ____________ very good business with your firm in the past.

33. My grandparents ____________ a long voyage around the world last year. It ____________ them a lot of good.

34. We'll have to ____________ room for another bed. A new boy is coming next week.

35. I'm afraid we haven't ____________ any money yet. We'll have to ____________ something about it.

36. 'Can you ____________ room for me in the car?' 'Sorry, but there's no room for anybody else.'

37. 'Mum, when are you going to ____________ dinner?' 'In a minute. Let me finish what I am ____________.'

38. Children, what are you ____________ ? Don't ____________ so much noise.'

39. 'I am going to ____________ a shelf for all these books.' 'Let me ____________ something to help you.'

40. 'Why don't you ____________ some coffee.' 'OK, I'll ____________ some.'

DO · MAKE (CONT.)

1. If the Prime Minister .... a speech, don't believe him. He hasn't .... anything to solve our problems.
2. 'What a wonderful idea. Let's .... an apple pie.' 'No, let's .... a rice pudding.'
3. What awful weather this is! Let's .... some tea.' 'OK, let's .... as you say.'
4. 'How beautiful! Did you .... that little boat yourself?' 'Yes, I .... it all by myself.'
5. She was going to .... a fire in the fireplace and bring some coal but she had no matches and she didn't .... anything.
6. If we don't hurry we'll never .... dinner by seven o'clock. We'll have to .... an effort.'
7. Come on, boys. We'll have to .... this place clean before the sergeant comes.
8. 'Who goes there? Don't .... a movement or I'll shoot.' 'Don't shoot, I'm not .... anything.'
9. 'That's a nice sweater you are .... , who is it for?' 'For nobody. I'm .... all this work for nothing, really.'
10. 'Do they .... their own clothes in that shop?' 'No, they don't .... any work in that shop.'
11. 'Have you ever .... a French omelette with six eggs?' 'No, I've never .... such a thing.'
12. 'Is there anything to .... in this place?' 'There's nothing to .... but you can .... friends with the country people.'
13. 'Why don't you tell your children to stop .... that awful noise?' 'Well, there is not much I can .... about it.'
14. 'This son of yours .... friends easily, doesn't he?' 'Yes, he certainly ....'
15. 'I like .... the housework, and you?' 'Well, I don't like .... the beds.'
16. 'How often do you .... the ironing in this house?' 'Well, we usually .... the ironing once a week.'
17. I'm going to my room to .... some reading. Can you .... something to eat for me?
18. 'Who is going to .... the cooking, boys?' 'Well, I'm not going to .... it that's for sure.'
19. Both, my wife and my daughter have .... their hair this morning at home.
20. There's a slogan that says «............ love, don't .... war», and I say «let's .... peace as well».

21. The women? Well, neither has ____________ the washing yet. I'll have to ____________ it myself.'

22. I've got to ____________ a couple of jobs before going home. Can you ____________ me a favour and tell my wife?

23. 'How long have you been ____________ that, Mary?' 'Well, I've been ____________ it for two hours.'

24. Take this medicine. It will ____________ you a lot of good. Take it and don't ____________ trouble.

25. 'You haven't ____________ much work lately, have you?' 'No, I haven't ____________ anything yet.'

26. 'That man has ____________ me a very good service.' 'Well, I'm sure that he will ____________ you pay for it.'

27. You'll have to ____________ better than that, I'm afraid. That won't ____________.

28. The teacher told me to ____________ the homework again. He ____________ me ____________ it again.'

29. 'You must ____________ good to other people.' 'I am always ____________ favours!'

30. 'Did you ____________ your breathing exercises?' 'No, I haven't ____________ them yet.'

31. 'You are ____________ a lot of things wrong.' 'Well, I'm sure I'm ____________ something right.'

32. 'You've ____________ a very good job, congratulations.' 'Thank you, you ____________ me very happy.'

33. 'We're going to ____________ a nice trip this weekend.' 'Why don't you ____________ me a favour. Let me come with you.'

34. 'It has been a pleasure to ____________ business with you' 'Yes, we'll have to ____________ an effort and ____________ more business in future.'

35. You must all ____________ much more work than you are ____________ at the moment, children.'

36. He is going to ____________ a good doctor. Don't ____________ a mistake about it.

37. 'What are you ________?' 'I'm ____________ bread. This bread is ____________ of wheat and that one is ____________ of rye.'

38. 5 and 5 ____________ 10, and 2 times 4 ____________ 8.

39. Well, I don't think that he is as bad as you ____________ him out to be.

40. 'Don't ____________ that. You are ____________ a fool of yourself.'

Fill in the gaps 1

CAN · COULD · TO BE ABLE

1. The problem is so difficult that not even Tom .... understand it.
2. '.............. you do it alone?' 'No, I .... do it alone.'
3. 'Will you .... to come tonight?' 'No, I won't .... to come.'
4. '.............. you play the piano when you were eight?' 'No, I .... play the piano until I was 10.'
5. '.............. you come to the meeting?' 'No, I don't think we ....'
6. '.............. you speak English when you were a child?' 'No, I .... speak English when I was a child.
7. 'Will they .... to do it on Monday?' 'No, they won't .... to do it until Tuesday.'
8. '.............. you do me a favour?' 'Yes, of course I .... do you a favour.'
9. 'Have you done it?' 'No, I haven't .... to do it yet.'
10. '.............. you play the piano?' 'Well, I .... when I was a child, but I haven't .... to practise for years.'
11. '.............. your sister swim?' 'No, she ...., but she is going to learn.'
12. I haven't .... to finish in time, I am afraid.
13. '.............. you speak Chinese when you were a child, Mr Chang?' 'No, I ....; I was born in England.'
14. I looked for the book everywhere but I .... find it.
15. I haven't .... to sleep very well lately.'
16. He kept on talking, but I .... hardly understand what he was saying.
17. '.............. your sister cook when she got married?' 'No, she .... very well.'
18. When I was seventeen I .... run a hundred metres in 11 seconds.
19. 'Have you done what I asked you?' 'No, I haven't .... to do it yet.'
20. 'Will you go to the meeting tonight?' 'No, I won't .... to go.'

21. '__________ you type?' 'Well, I __________ when I was younger, but I __________ type very well now.'

22. 'Will you __________ to help him?' 'No, I don't think I'll __________ to help him.'

23. 'I haven't __________ to come before because there was a traffic hold up on the motorway.'

24. If you hurry you will __________ to arrive on time for the meeting.'

25. Only two years studying and he __________ already speak English fluently.'

26. 'What __________ we do in Paris during the two weeks?' 'We __________ do a lot of things.'

27. I don't know if I will __________ to come this afternoon.

28. 'Have you finished repairing the TV set?' 'No, I haven't __________ to finish it yet.'

29. A year ago I __________ understand a word of French. Now I __________ understand quite a lot.

30. 'How fast __________ you type, Mary?' 'Well, I __________ type a hundred words a minute.'

31. At this speed we will never __________ to arrive in time for the Conference.'

32. 'Have you read the news?' 'No, I haven't __________ to read the paper yet.'

33. '__________ you swim when you were a child?' 'Yes, I __________ swim when I was four.'

34. 'At what time will I __________ to have my car?' 'You'll __________ to take it away in the afternoon.'

35. '__________ you tell me the time, please?' 'Sorry, I __________, I haven't got a watch.'

36. 'I'm deeply sorry I haven't __________ to be of any help to you.'

37. '__________ you come with us?' 'Well, I __________ go if you asked me.'

38. 'If you give me money I'll probably __________ to buy it for you this afternoon.'

39. 'Have you spoken to little Jimmy?' 'No, I haven't __________ to speak to him yet.'

40. 'Have you read the book yet?' 'Well, I'll probably __________ to read it tonight.'

Fill in the gaps 1

AT · IN · ON

1. 'Where shall we meet?' 'Well, let's meet .... the station.'
2. 'Where were the boys?' 'They were .... the classroom.'
3. 'Where was the glass?' 'The glass was .... the table .... the hall.'
4. 'Where will you be tonight?' 'I'll be .... the club .... 9 o'clock.'
5. 'Did you hear a cat last night?' 'Yes, there was a cat .... the roof of my house.'
6. 'Where does your brother work?' 'Well, he works .... Bronson's.'
7. 'What are you looking at?' 'Well, did you see that big fish .... the water?, there, ... the river.'
8. 'Where's the picture I bought yesterday?' 'I hung it up. It is .... that wall.'
9. 'Do you live .... this street?' 'Yes, I live .... number 42.'
10. 'You are all wet, where have you been?' 'We've been walking .... the rain.'
11. 'When did it happen?' 'It happened .... Sunday morning.'
12. 'Did they come .... time?' 'No, they arrived late .... the meeting.'
13. 'It was very difficult to do that .... the past.' 'And it's very difficult to do it .... present.'
14. 'When are they coming?' 'They will come .... the 20th of September.'
15. 'Hello, Mary. Are the children .... home?' 'No, they are .... school.'
16. 'When did you come to live here?' 'We came to live here .... 1990.'
17. 'Did you have a look .... the list?' 'Yes, and I can see that my name is not .... it.'
18. 'Were you .... Oxford university?' 'Yes, I was .... university from 1985 to 1990.'
19. 'When do you watch television?' 'We usually watch TV .... the evening, after tea.'
20. The train was .... the station, and there were many passengers .... the train.'

21. Take the London train and change .... Crewe. The train for Cardiff leaves .... 2.35.

22. 'Did you arrive .... time for the concert?' 'Yes, we arrived .... time to buy the tickets.'

23. My house is .... the right, the Robinsons' is .... the left.

24. You can see the stars .... night and sometimes .... the evening.'

25. The little girl had oil .... her hair and .... her face.'

26. 'Somebody told me that you came late.' '............... the contrary, we came very early.'

27. 'What do you do .... the weekends?' Well, ... weekdays we stay at home, but .... the weekends we go out.'

28. 'Look .... that mirror, shall we buy it?' 'Yes, but I'll look .... myself .... it first.'

29. I wouldn't like to meet these people, and .... the other hand I'm very busy .... the moment.'

30. Can you read a car number plate .... 50 metres?' 'I can read it .... 80 metres.'

31. There was a lot of snow .... the mountains, but very little .... the valleys.'

32. The passengers were waiting for a long time .... the plane before it took off.'

33. I didn't understand it .... the beginning, but .... the end I could understand him very well.'

34. He took the uncut diamond and looked .... it carefully .... the light.'

35. 'My office is .... the first floor.' Well, mine is .... the second.'

36. All his tools were .... hand. They were .... the bench.'

37. There were millions of birds .... the sky. The sun was setting .... the horizon.

38. Have you seen the blood stains .... the ceiling, ... the walls and .... the carpet?'

39. The Romans were always .... war with their neighbours. Their armies were never .... peace or .... rest.'

40. There was something strange .... that scene, and .... the way people behaved.'

Fill in the gaps 1

AT · IN · ON (CONT.)

1. 'Where's Bath?' 'Well, Bath is a small town .... the road to Bristol.'
2. 'Have you been .... holiday?' 'Yes, but I was getting bored .... the end of it.'
3. 'Can I pay by cheque?' 'No, sorry. All these items have to paid .... cash.'
4. 'Did he do it .... purpose?' 'Of course he did it .... purpose.'
5. 'Where are the Evans this morning?' 'Well, they are all .... church.'
6. 'That man likes to speak .... a loud voice.' 'Well, he told me that .... a very low voice.'
7. Everything he said is written .... this page. It's all written .... ink.
8. 'Where does she live?' 'She lives .... London Avenue, ... 27 London Avenue.'
9. The old mansion .... the hill had been .... ruins for years.
10. 'Did you walk to the station?' 'Yes, we went there .... foot.'
11. I want everything .... hand; not .... the drawer.
12. Don't put the book .... the shelf; put it .... the trunk.
13. She was .... the baker's buying bread.
14. I'll meet you .... the station, ... the waiting-room.
15. 'There's a lot of traffic .... this road.' 'Well, there are a lot of cars .... the streets.'
16. There was a little cottage .... the coast.
17. Stop .... the first traffic lights you see .... town.
18. 'Are you good .... football?' 'Well, I was never very good .... sports.'
19. They are working .... the road. They have been .... work since 8 o'clock this morning.'
20. That happened .... times of war. Now we are .... a time of peace.'

21. .... this street there are several houses .... sale.'

22. This boy is very bad .... mathematics but very good .... football.'

23. When they got home they found the jug .... the floor .... pieces.

24. The train has arrived .... time, if we hurry we'll get there .... time for the conference.'

25. She spent hours .... the window looking .... the passers-by.

26. All the children were .... school. They were .... their classrooms. They were .... good health.

27. 'Goodbye, children. I'll see you .... Saturday. Be good.'

28. That son of yours is very clever .... solving crossword puzzles.

29. All the children were sitting .... a circle around the old man.

30. The man wore a hat .... his head. There was a feather .... the hat.

31. There was a strange-looking man .... the door. He was dressed .... black.

32. Get to one side, we are .... a hurry. There is somebody .... danger.

33. She had a diamond ring .... her finger and a gold bracelet .... her wrist.

34. 'Where is he staying?' 'He's staying .... the Grand Hotel, ... High Street.'

35. He was dressed .... a dark grey suit and wore a sort of cloak .... his shoulders.

36. 'I saw that film .... television.' 'Did you? I saw it .... the cinema.'

37. I didn't know anything about it .... that time, but .... the time of the murder I was .... New York.

38. My boss was .... a bad mood, so I didn't ask him for a rise.

40. 'Where did you hear the news?' 'I heard it .... the radio.

AT · IN · ON (CONT.)

1. 'Where were you when they called you?' ' .... the moment they called me I was .... garden.'
2. The family live .... poverty .... the outskirts of the town.
3. 'What do you do .... weekdays?' 'I work, but .... the weekend I rest.'
4. She always arrives late .... the office. She never comes .... time.
5. He was a tall man .... his fifties. His hair was greying .... the sides.
6. We all get together .... Christmas, especially .... Christmas day.
7. I am .... your service, Madam. You can place your trust .... me.
8. He had a piece of bread .... his right hand and a bottle of water .... his left hand.
9. The house was .... fire when we arrived. The firemen were already .... the way.
10. My son is .... the Navy. He is .... sea .... the moment. He is .... a very good ship.
11. He played the match .... place of his brother who was ill .... bed with flu.
12. 'What I told you is .... page 2.' 'I thought it was .... the front page.'
13. They were all sitting down .... table for dinner .... the dining-room.
14. .... view of his success last year he is back .... town this year.
15. The soldier was .... duty all night .... the guardroom.
16. 'Was he sitting .... the front?' 'No, he was sitting .... the back.'
17. The young couple walked happily hand .... hand .... the park. Then, they sat down .... a bench.
18. There were houses .... both sides of the road. They stood .... a row.
19. 'Were you .... Frank's party?' 'Yes, we were there .... nine o'clock.'
20. There were about fifty people .... the room .... silence.

AT · IN · ON (CONT.)

21. My father is .... the committee now. He's been .... the party for 20 years.

22. They were going .... full speed. They didn't stop .... the traffic lights.

23. They had been fighting for weeks, but the end was clearly .... sight now.

24. My grandfather wrote a book .... English literature .... 1966.

25. 'I'll see you .... midday.' Sorry, I won't be here .... noon. I'll be back .... midnight.'

26. The car is .... good condition, and they are selling it .... a good price.

27. 'Have you got any money .... you?' 'Sorry, I haven't got any money .... me.'

28. 'I saw Mrs. Brian .... the hypermarket. She was .... the food section.

29. There were many sheep .... the field. They were lying .... the grass.

30. I telephoned him .... New Year's day, but he wasn't ....

31. We were .... breakfast when the postman came with our mail.

32. There are very few cars .... this car park. Most people leave their cars .... the street.

33. What is on .... the cinema tonight?' A very good film is .... at the Odeon.

34. The car was going .... about 80 kilometres an hour when it rushed head .... against the truck.

35. My father was .... the living room and my mother was .... the kitchen.

36. Put a stamp .... the envelope. I'll drop the letter .... the letterbox .... my way to work.

37. The books were .... his bag, and his bag was .... his shoulders.

38. I always have you .... my mind. You are always .... my thoughts.

39. I'll see you .... your birthday. Will there be many people .... your birthday party?

40. I was .... the bus. I saw him .... his new car. His wife was .... the back seat.

AT · IN · ON (CONT.)

1. I was born .... 1958, ... June 16th. My wife was born .... winter, the same year.
2. My grandmother died .... the age of ninety .... 1995, ... a spring day.
3. Life was very difficult .... the middle ages. Most people lived .... poverty.
4. We are working very hard .... present. We have 40 employees .... the moment.
5. 'Where were you last year?' 'Last year .... April we were .... London.'
6. I can run a hundred metres .... eleven seconds. I'll run .... the Stadium .... Saturday afternoon.
7. That girl has run a thousand metres .... four minutes and two seconds.
8. My daughter was very happy .... her wedding day. She wore the wedding ring .... her finger.
9. The book will be finished .... forty days' time, ... July.
10. We will be there .... about 10 o'clock .... the morning.
11. 'I'll see you .... lunch time.' 'Sorry, I won't be .... lunchtime. I'll arrive .... dinner time.'
12. .... that time people were very poor. They lived .... misery.
13. Most people .... England like to relax .... the weekends. They work enough .... weekdays.
14. .... this country trains always arrive .... time.
15. All the passengers arrived .... time for the ferry. The ferry left .... time.
16. Paris is beautiful .... spring. Many tourists go to the French capital .... April and June.
17. The best thing is to go .... Saturday. There are not so many people .... the weekend.
18. They got married .... 1980 and divorced .... 1985. They lived .... an endless quarrel for five years.
19. Most people usually work .... their gardens .... Sunday mornings.'
20. We always have a party .... New Year's eve. There were a lot of people .... the last party.

AT · IN · ON (CONT.)

21. My father will retire .... a few years' time. He'll retire .... the age of 65.

22. If everybody speaks .... the same time nobody will understand each other.

23. If you sleep during the day you won't be able to sleep .... night.

24. We always go out for dinner .... our wedding anniversary. It is .... the second of June.

25. I went to bed .... midnight and got up .... six o'clock in the morning.

26. 'Where was Shakespeare born?' 'He was born .... Stratford .... 1564.

27. The old woman died .... 1995, ... the age of 95. She was born .... the beginning of the century.

28. Both trains are leaving .... the same time, ... five minutes.

29. George started school .... five and left it .... sixteen.

30. 'Was America discovered .... 1492?' 'Yes, ... October, ... October 12th 1492.'

31. 'When are you coming?' 'I'll be there .... ten minutes, ... a quarter to ten.'

32. I'll come to see you .... Tuesday morning, ... eleven.

33. The course starts .... October 4th and ends .... June 20th.

34. Columbus arrived .... Lisbon .... 1476 and married Felipa Perestrello .... 1478.

35. .... September 10th they saw birds. At 10 o'clock .... the morning .... October 12th 1492 they arrived .... the New World.

36. '.............. which epoch does the story take place?' '.............. the Middle Ages. Life was difficult .... that time.'

37. He was born .... London, ... spring. His mother died .... his birth.

38. He lived .... the streets .... the age of twelve.

39. .... 1592 Shakespeare was well established .... the theatre. His company acted .... the Globe Theatre .... Christmas.

40. He married Anne Hathaway .... 1582, ... the age of eighteen.

Fill in the gaps 1

WOULD

1. If we had a car we .... on holiday to the Costa Brava. (go)
2. 'What .... you .... if you had a lot of money?' 'I .... to Miami.' (do) (go)
3. If my son passed all his exams he .... with us to Benidorm.' (come)
4. If we went on holiday to Spain we .... an apartment in Salou. (rent)
5. '.................................... you .... to a hotel if you couldn't rent an apartment? (go)
6. If we went by car we .... several times on the way. (stop)
7. '.................................... you .... all night if you were in a hurry?' 'No, I .... all night.' (drive)
8. If we drove all night we .... in the morning. (arrive)
9. If we went to the Hotel Paraíso we .... very near the beach. (be)
10. If there was a swimming pool in the hotel I .... in the sea. (swim)
11. If you sold your house in Croydon you .... a lot of money. (get)
12. '.................................... you .... the house if you had money?' 'No, I .... it even if I had money.' (buy)
13. If you bought that house, ... you .... to live in this town? (come)
14. If I came to live in this town I .... a school for my children. (look for)
15. If the children went to another school they .... new friends. (make)
16. '.................................... you .... near your job if you lived in this house?'
'No, I .... near my new job.' (be)
17. I .... to that shopping centre if I could go to this one.' (go)
18. If you went by car you .... problems parking in that street. (have)
19. '.................................... you .... by bus if you had a car?' 'No, I .... by bus.' (go)
20. I think it .... cheaper if I went to the office by underground.' (be)

21. 'Jeremy said that he .... you some money if you needed it.' 'Tell him that I .... any money from him.' (lend) (take)
22. What .... you .... if you won a million pounds, Jennifer? (do)
23. Ann was half an hour late, even though she promised me she .... never .... late again. (be)
24. 'If you found a £10 note in the street, ... you .... it?' (keep)
25. '.............................. you .... hunting in this weather?' 'No, I .... hunting in any weather.' (go)
26. '.............................. you .... to see that film?' 'No, I .... to see it.' (like)
27. 'Do you think the children .... to see that film?' 'No, I don't think they ....' (like)
28. '.............................. you .... in the marathon if you were fit?' 'No, I .... 26 miles.' (run)
29. I .... photographs in the theatre if I were you. It's forbidden. (take)
30. '.............................. your friend .... tonight if you asked him?' (come)
31. '.............................. you .... if I explained it slowly?' 'Yes, I .... probably ....' (understand)
32. If I were you I .... litter in the street. You'll get a fine. (drop)
33. 'What .... you .... if you lost your passport in a foreign country?' 'I .... to the police.' (do) (go)
34. 'If a film star asked you to marry him/her, what .... you ....?' 'I .... no.' (do) (say)
35. I .... to the speed limit if I were you. There is a police car behind. (keep)
36. If we caught the 8.30 train we .... too early for the party. (be)
37. What .... if you didn't go to work next Monday?' '.............................. your boss .... angry?' (happen) (be)
38. What .... you .... if the public threw eggs at you in the theatre? (do)
39. 'If you were offered the job, ... you .... it?' 'Yes, I .... probably .... it.' (take)
40. If you didn't live so far away we .... you more often. (visit)

Fill in the gaps 1

IMPERATIVE

1. Children, ________ with me to the sitting-room. Don't ________ to the garden. It's cold. (come) (go out)
2. Mrs. Brown, ________ with your daughter this afternoon. Don't ________ tomorrow. (come)
3. 'Your friend is waiting for you.' 'Well, ________ him ________ ' (wait)
4. 'I am going to Paris next week.' 'Oh, ________ me ________ to Paris with you.' (go)
5. 'I am hungry. Can I have something to eat?' 'Yes, ________ down and ________ ' (sit) (eat)
6. Jimmy, ________ everything on the plate. Don't ________ anything. (eat) (leave)
7. It's very late. ________ us ________, boys. Don't ________ there doing nothing. (hurry) (stand)
8. 'Look, Mary. ________ us ________ at this hotel.' 'No, don't ________ us ________ here.' (stay)
9. '________ us ________ at the underground station at seven.' 'No, ________ us ________ at 7.30 at the Odeon Theatre.' (meet)
10. '________ this letter, Jennifer. Don't ________ those two letters.' (type)
11. Don't ________ the ironing, Mary. ________ Nora ________ it. (do)
12. ________ David to get up. Don't ________ him ________ in bed all morning.' (tell) (lie)
13. '________ me ________ with you to the cinema tonight' 'OK, ________ Lucy ________ with us too.' (go) (come)
14. '________ at that fence!' '________ us ________ to the Jones about that!' (look) (speak)
15. 'OK, ________ the workmen ________ to my office. I want to talk to them.' (come)
16. Mary, don't ________ the beds yet; ________ the ironing. (make) (do)
17. Don't ________ to those children. Don't ________ them ________ us.' (speak) (see)
18. Don't ________ with those children. Don't ________ them ________ that to you. (play) (say)
19. ________ not ________ too early. ________ us ________ here a little longer. (go) (stay)
20. Don't ________ Charles ________ with us. Don't ________ him we are going. (come) (tell)

21. Judy is at the bus stop. Don't ____________ her ____________ you. Don't ____________ to her. (see) (speak)

22. ____________ Nelly ____________ a video tape when she comes. ____________ her to bring a video tape. (bring) (tell)

23. ____________ the boys to do it for you. ____________ them ____________ it for you. (tell) (do)

24. Johnny, don't ____________ that again. Don't ____________ me ____________ you do that again. (do) (see)

25. '____________ us ____________ the colours of the rooms.' 'No, ____________ not ____________ them.' (change)

26. 'Don't ____________ the colour of the bathroom.' 'Why not? ____________ us ____________ it.' (change)

27. Don't ____________ your mouth when you are eating. Don't ____________ me ____________ you open it. (open) (see)

28. It's too easy for them. ____________ them ____________ something more difficult. (do)

29. Don't ____________ to third gear yet. ____________ us ____________ a little more. (change) (practise)

30. Don't ____________ him where it is. ____________ him ____________ for it. (tell) (look)

31. ____________ us not ____________ them which house it is. ____________ them ____________ it. (tell) (guess)

32. ____________ Sylvia to ____________ here at once. I want to speak to her. (tell) (come)

33. ____________ us ____________ two seats at the Odeon. ____________ us ____________ that new film. (book) (see)

34. Don't ____________ them ____________ away. They've robbed the bank. (get)

35. ____________ us not ____________ . There is plenty of time. ____________ us ____________ a coffee. (hurry) (have)

36. Judy, ____________ this letter and ____________ it, please. Then ____________ it as soon as possible. (take) (type) (post)

37. ____________ the children ____________ to see me. ____________ them to come to see me. (come) (tell)

38. 'I think Mary is waiting for you.' 'Is she? well, ____________ her ____________ ' (wait)

39. ____________ us ____________ something more difficult today. ____________ us ____________ the Devil's Rock.' (do) (climb)

40. 'I think Bob is coming this way.' 'OK, ____________ him ____________.' (come)

Fill in the gaps 1
PASSIVE VOICE

1. This book .... by my father in 1980, when he was 50. (write)
2. These exercise .... at home by the children tonight. (do)
3. Flies .... always .... by spiders. Spiders .... never .... by flies. (kill)
4. These road works .... being .... by those men over there. (do)
5. All these boys and girls .... being .... by these teachers. (teach)
6. That firm .... in 1990 by this American multinational. (buy)
7. This TV set .... been .... by my brother. (repair)
8. This wonderful meal .... by this famous chef this morning. (prepare)
9. Florence .... one of the most beautiful cities in the world. (consider)
10. A foreign language .... not .... in 15 days. It takes years of hard work. (learn)
11. This film .... going to be .... all over the world. (see)
12. This book .... by this man in less than two months. (write)
13. All the milk .... been .... by the children. There is none left. (drink)
14. All things .... by God at the beginning of time. (make)
15. A lot of things .... by children playing at home. (break)
16. The horse .... by thunder and ran away before the man could get hold of it. (frighten)
17. Shakespeare .... to be the best playwright of all times. (consider)
18. I think it will be better if this job .... by my colleague. (do)
19. Those uniforms .... by these schoolboys next year. (wear)
20. The seat belts .... by the passengers on board the plane before it took off. (fasten)

21. All the jewels .... by the thieves during the night. (steal)

22. The beautiful blonde .... to a dance by the tall boy. (take)

23. A terrific goal .... by the centre forward just before half time. (score)

24. An invitation .... to us by the association for the blind. (send)

25. We .... tonight at the airport by Mr. Johnson and his wife tomorrow. (meet)

26. Many promises .... by the socialists when they came to power. (make)

27. All the beds .... by my mother every morning before breakfast. (make)

28. All the cakes .... by the children last night before going to bed. (eat)

29. All those buildings .... by fire after the earthquake. (destroy)

30. My house .... last night. Someone entered through the sitting-room window. (burgle)

31. Peter's car .... by the thieves during the night, and it .... in Brighton in the morning. (steal) (find)

32. The whole fish .... by the cat while we were watching television. (eat)

33. The homework .... by the children after tea tomorrow evening. (do)

34. This circular letter .... to all our clients by mistake. (send)

35. 'They say many things about that.' 'Yes, many things .... about that.' (say)

36. 'We'll see that film.' 'Yes, that film .... by us.'

37. 'My brother would do it.' 'So, it .... by your brother, then' (do)

38. All the injured .... to hospital by passing motorists. (take)

39. Mrs. Smith .... by Mrs. Owl that her husband had entered Mrs. Brown's house. (inform)

40. In this firm many things .... for exporting.Many other things .... for the home market. (make)

Fill in the gaps 1

MUST · HAVE TO

1. Sorry, Mary, I'm afraid I .... go now. It's very late and I .... to catch the train.
2. 'Oh, dear, ... you go so early?' 'Yes, I .... be in London before 10 o'clock.'
3. 'Do you .... to go on this business trip?' 'Yes, I'm afraid I'll .... to.'
4. Jimmy, you're eating too fast. You .... eat so fast. It's not good for you.
5. Little babies .... be kept warm at all times. They .... catch a cold.
6. You .... give it to me as soon as possible. We .... to post it this morning.
7. 'What .... you do when you get up in the morning?' 'I .... wash my face and clean my teeth.'
8. Boys, you .... ask so many silly questions. You .... think before opening your mouth.
9. Little children .... study too much. They .... be able to play.
10. We'll .... to buy some more books. I'm afraid we haven't got enough.
11. You .... take these things to the office as soon as you can. You'll .... to make sure that they are there by tomorrow.
12. It's going to be very windy tonight. All the windows .... be shut before we leave.
13. Children, you .... shout in class. You .... sit quietly at your desks.
14. 'Well, girls. What .... you do in case of fire?' 'We .... to get out of the building quickly.'
15. 'Jimmy, ... you stay at home every Sunday?' 'Why don't you go out with your friends?' 'Ok, Mum. I'll go out if I .... to.'
16. Don't drink like that, Johnny. You .... drink so fast. You .... eat and drink slowly.
17. You'll .... to run much faster if you want to win. You .... go so slowly.
18. I .... to stay at home yesterday because I wasn't feeling very well. I'll .... to go to the doctor today.
19. If you want to pass your exams you'll .... to work hard for the next two weeks.
20. 'Look at John. He .... be waiting for his girlfriend.' 'Well, he'll .... to wait for quite a bit. She's still in bed.'

21. 'If you want to win the match you'll .... to score a goal as soon as possible.' Yes, we'll .... to score a goal soon.'
22. 'Children, you .... say those things about the teachers.' 'Why .... we?'
23. '.............. I take this medicine?' 'Yes, you'll .... to drink it all. Doctor's orders.'
24. The goods will .... to be in Porstmouth by next month. We'll .... to hurry things up.
25. Children, you .... open your mouth when you are eating. It's bad manners.
26. 'You .... say anything unless you're absolutely sure.' 'What .... I do then?'
27. 'Will you .... to go to Rome this weekend?' 'Yes, I .... be there before 10 o'clock on Saturday morning.'
28. Goodbye, everyone. I .... go now. I .... catch the train to Bristol.
29. .... you say those things in front of everybody? Do you .... to keep saying those things again and again?
30. 'Oh, Frank. .... you stay in bed all Sunday morning?' 'Well, I don't .... to go out until after dinner.'
31. You'll .... to be careful if you don't want to have an accident. The roads are very slippery.
32. In this country boys and girls .... stay at school until they are 16.
33. I would .... to tell the teacher if you didn't do all your homework.
34. You .... say those things. You will .... to apologize to that old lady.
35. This year I'll .... to study very hard. I .... pass all my exams in June.
36. Yesterday I .... to go to Jimmy's school. I .... to talk to his teacher.
37. You don't .... to wait for us, Mum.
38. 'We .... put the prices up.' 'Yes, we'll .... to raise the prices.'
39. 'Yesterday I .... to go to see my boss?' 'Did you .... to?
40. You don't .... to pay now. You can take it home now and pay later.

COMPARATIVES · SUPERLATIVES

1. 'Is your grandfather's house very big?' 'Yes, it is .... than mine.' (big)
2. That old castle is much .... than Buckingham Palace. It is the .... palace in England. (old)
3. Peter is .... than John. He is the .... boy in his class. (tall)
4. This girl is .... than my sister. She is the .... girl in her school. (small)
5. My home town is the .... in this country. It is much .... than yours. (nice)
6. Today it is .... than it was yesterday. It is the .... of the year. (warm)
7. My son works .... than most boys at school. He is the .... working boy in the school. (hard)
8. Her illness was much .... than we at first thought. (serious)
9. Could you speak .... please? You speak much .... than my teacher. (slowly) (fast)
10. If you are tired in the mornings try to go to bed .... (early)
11. This jacket is much .... than that one. I need a .... size. Show me the .... you have in the shop. (small) (large)
12. If you lived .... I would go to see you .... (near) (often)
13. This hotel is .... than that one. I thought it would be much .... (cheap) (expensive)
14. This flat is .... than ours. We need something much .... (small) (big)
15. This armchair is much .... than that one. It's the .... armchair in the shop. (comfortable)
16. My mother looks much .... than she is. She looks the .... woman of all. (young)
17. My toothache is .... today than it was yesterday. (painful)
18. There were a lot of people on the bus. It was .... than usual. (crowded)
19. She's .... than her sister. She is the .... girl I have ever seen. (beautiful)
20. This book is .... than mine. It is the .... book I have ever studied. (difficult)

21. That girl looks very healthy. She looks ______________ than her sister. (healthy)

22. The visit to this country was ______________ than I expected (interesting)

23. My exam was ______________ than yours. It was the ______________ exam I ever had. (easy)

24. Yesterday was ______________ than last Sunday. It was the ______________ day of the year. (hot)

25. I think this is the ______________ film I have ever seen. (boring)

26. My hotel is ______________ than yours. It was the ______________ hotel I could find. (cheap)

27. She is one of the ______________ persons I have ever known. She is one of the ______________ I've ever met. (nice) (pleasant)

28. My ______________ child was 14 years old last week, and my ______________ one was 5 yesterday. (old) (young)

29. 'Which is the ______________ river in England?' 'The Thames I think. It's ______________ than the Cam, anyway.' (long)

30. He is very dangerous. He is the ______________ criminal in this country. (dangerous)

31. It was a very bad experience. It was one of the ______________ experiences in my life. (bad)

32. He plays ______________ than Bronson. He is the ______________ tennis player in the club. (good)

33. This is the ______________ story that I have ever heard. (extraordinary)

34. Football is the ______________ sport in this country. it's ______________ than rugby. (popular)

35. This problem is ______________ than yours. It's the ______________ problem I have ever solved. (difficult)

36. My joke was ______________ than yours. It was the ______________ joke that I have ever told. (funny)

37. This bed is ______________ than yours. It's the ______________ bed I have ever slept in. (uncomfortable)

38. My wedding day was one of the ______________ days in my life. (happy)

39. It was a very bad mistake. It was one of the ______________ mistakes that I have ever made. (bad)

40. This drink was very sweet. It was the ______________ drink that I have ever had. (sweet)

Fill in the gaps 1

YET · STILL

1. Jimmy is .... in bed sleeping. He hasn't woken up ....
2. We are .... waiting for his reply. He hasn't replied ....
3. The concert hasn't finished .... It's .... going on.
4. They are .... thinking about what colour to paint the sitting-room. They haven't decided ....
5. My grandfather .... plays tennis, though he doesn't play football any more.
6. 'Haven't you finished writing that letter .... ?' 'No, I haven't finished .... I'm .... writing it.'
7. 'Does your father .... work in that factory?' 'Yes, he .... works there.
8. George is .... here. He hasn't gone back to England ....
9. 'Haven't you finished correcting .... ?' 'No, I'm .... correcting exercises.
10. 'Does old McDonald .... drink so much?' 'Yes, he .... drinks quite a lot.'
11. 'Are you .... growing a beard?' 'Yes, I haven't shaved ....'
12. 'Hasn't it stopped raining .... ?' 'No, it is .... raining.'
13. 'Haven't you had your dinner .... ?' 'I haven't finished .... I'm .... eating it.'
14. 'Haven't you read the letter .... ?' 'No, I'm .... reading it.'
15. 'Are you .... painting that picture?' 'Well, I haven't quite finished ....'
16. 'Haven't they filled in the forms .... ?' 'No, they haven't finished .... They are .... filling them in.'
17. He hasn't come out of hospital .... , he is .... there.
18. 'Can't you drive a car .... ?' 'No, I am .... learning.'
19. 'Hasn't Mary brushed her hair .... ?' 'No, she is .... washing it.'
20. 'Can't you speak French .... Jimmy?' 'No, I am .... learning it.'

21. Have you finished ....?' 'No, we are .... working.'

22. 'Have the children had their breakfast ....?' 'No, they are .... having it.'

23. Johnny is .... in the bathroom. He hasn't finished washing ....

24. You .... smoke, do you? Haven't you given it up ....?

25. What! Are you .... eating? Haven't you finished eating ....?

26. My father hasn't finished reading his paper ...., he's .... reading it.

27. 'Do you .... live in the same old house?' 'Yes; we haven't moved .... '

28. 'I'm hungry. Is dinner ready ....?' 'No; I'm .... preparing it.'

29. My friend Jack is .... unemployed. He hasn't found a job ....

30. 'Are you .... thinking about it?' 'Yes, I haven't made a decision ....'

31. My children are .... studying French. They can't speak fluently ....

32. I can't give the picture to you ...., I am .... painting it.

33. We haven't taken a holiday this year .... We are .... thinking about the date and the place.

34. 'I have never asked for advice ....' 'So, you are .... too proud to ask for any advice.'

35. Jimmy, don't go ...., you haven't told me what happened ....

36. Your son is .... washing the car. He hasn't finished washing it ....

37. If we hurry we can .... arrive on time. We mustn't despair ....

38. My father is .... writing that book. He has been writing it for two years and hasn't finished it ....

39. I haven't spoken to him .... He .... doesn't know about it.

40. 'Haven't you taken the medicine ....?' 'No, I'm .... preparing it.'

Fill in the gaps 1

DURING · FOR · SINCE · AGO

1. I haven't seen Gabriel .... Christmas and that was six months ....
2. I came here 20 years .... , so you can say that I have been here .... 20 years.
3. 'I haven't seen your brother .... three months.' 'Haven't you? I saw him .... the rehearsal.'
4. 'I spoke to your sister .... the interval.' 'Did you? I haven't seen her .... 5 o'clock.'
5. We haven't met .... our last holidays, about eight months ....
6. I went to the dentist two years .... I haven't been there .... then.
7. He was walking up and down .... hours .... the night.
8. I stayed there .... two months and many things happened .... that time.
9. 'It was very cold .... the night.' 'Yes, and very hot .... the day.'
10. We haven't been to London .... 1990. We were there .... two weeks then.
11. I studied Greek many years .... I studied it .... three years.
12. I haven't seen Francis .... Monday. I was with him .... five minutes .... the meeting.
13. She's been working here .... April. So, she's been working with us .... about six months.
14. I told him that months .... I haven't seen him .... then.
15. 'You haven't washed that car .... months.' 'Well, I washed it two months .... '
16. Your sister has been making up her face .... half an hour. She entered the bathroom thirty minutes ....
17. The telephone rang several times .... the meal. That was two hours ....
18. 'I have been doing the same job .... 1990.' 'You started in this firm six years .... , didn't you?
19. 'I last saw him 10 years .... ' 'You haven't seen him .... ten years?'
20. 'She has been waiting for him .... three years.' 'She has been waiting for him .... he left, hasn't she?

DURING · FOR · SINCE · AGO

21. There are two intervals .... the performance. The show goes on .... four hours.

22. People have been coming .... five o'clock in the morning. They've been coming .... hours.

23. They've lived in this house .... five or six years. I think they came here six years ....

24. Two injured men have been taken to hospital .... the night.

25. Many people have emigrated to Australia .... 1940. Thousands went there .... the war.

26. I was just speaking to him a few minutes .... We were speaking .... twenty minutes.

27. 'I haven't seen him .... the last two months.' 'I know you haven't seen him .... September.'

28. It's very hot in here .... the summer. The heat is scorching .... three months.

29. 'We haven't been here .... Easter.' 'Yes, I know you haven't been here .... six months.'

30. 'He was here two minutes .... ' 'Was he? Well, I haven't seen him .... ages.'

31. I met a very nice girl .... my stay on the island. We went out together .... weeks.

32. Somebody came to see us .... the rehearsal. He was watching us .... half an hour.

33. He has been working with us .... five years. He first came five years ....

34. 'It was cold .... the night, wasn't it?' 'Yes, it's been very cold .... the last six or seven days.'

35. I haven't seen Peter .... Jane's birthday party. And that was six weeks ....

36. 'I went to the doctor two months .... ' 'Yes, I knew you hadn't been to the doctor .... two months.'

37. She studied piano composition many years ....

38. They have been meeting secretly .... years, ever .... they met five years ....

39. The two politicians have met three or four times .... the year.

40. .... the election campaign they threw insults at each other. They haven't spoken to each other .... months.

Fill in the gaps 1

QUESTION TAGS

1. 'You are a very tall man, ...?' 'Yes, but I am not very heavy, ...'
2. 'The Browns have a very nice house, ...?' 'Yes, but it's not very big, ...?'
3. 'You speak Italian, ...?' 'Yes, but I don't speak it well, ...'.
4. 'You can do better than that, ...?' 'I'm sorry but I can't do it much better, ...?'
5. 'She could cook very well, ...?' 'Yes, she was a very good cook, ...?'
6. 'She is a very pretty woman, ...?' 'Yes, but she is not very intelligent, ...?'
7. 'You come here every Sunday, ...?' 'Yes, but we have never met before, ...?'
8. 'Caroline plays tennis very well, ...?' 'Yes, but she doesn't play as well as her sister, ...?'
9. She learnt a lot when she was in the USA, ...?' 'Yes, but she didn't learn enough, ...?'
10. You will come with us, ...?' 'Yes, I'll go, but Peter won't be coming, ...?'
11. 'You would do it better, ...?' 'Yes, but it would never be perfect, ...?'
12. 'There is a lot of water, ...?' 'Yes, but there is not enough, ...?'
13. 'There are a lot of people, ...?' 'Yes, but there are not too many, ...?'
14. 'She sings very well, ...?' 'Yes, but she doesn't sing well enough to be a professional singer, ...?'
15. 'He speaks Japanese, ...?' 'Yes, but he doesn't speak very well, ...?'
16. 'Your friend ran in the marathon, ...?' 'Yes, but he didn't run very well, ...?'
17. 'They will come on Sunday, ...?' 'Yes, but they won't come too early, ...?'
18. 'We must take him to hospital, ...?' 'Yes, but we mustn't rush, ...?'
19. 'The hotel was very expensive, ...?' 'Yes, but it wasn't very comfortable, ...?'
20. 'You have a good car, ...?' 'Yes, but it doesn't look very expensive, ...?'

21. 'He is not an engineer, ...?' 'No, but he looks like one, ...?'
22. 'That girl is not coming with you, ...?' 'No, she isn't. She's very pretty, ...?'
23. You haven't got a German car, ...?' 'No; but I've got a very good Italian car, ...?'
24. 'You can't drive yet, ...?' 'No, but I can learn, ...?'
25. 'You haven't given the meat to the cat, ...?' 'Well, I haven't got a cat, ...?'
26. 'You don't speak French, ...?' 'No, I don't. But you speak it very well, ...?'
27. 'The TV doesn't give a good picture, ...?' 'No, but we can repair it, ...?'
28. 'There are not many pictures here, ...?' 'No, but the pictures are very good, ...?'
29. 'She won't pass her exam, ...?' 'Perhaps not, but she will try, ...?'
30. 'You wouldn't do it, ...?' 'No, I wouldn't, but I could try, ...?'
31. 'You haven't finished it yet, ...?' 'No, but I have done most of it, ...?'
32. 'It won't rain this afternoon, ...?' 'No, but it will be cloudy, ...?'
33. 'They wouldn't do it very well, ...?' 'No, but perhaps they would do it better than me, ...?'
34. 'You won't come next Sunday, ...?' 'No, but you will let me come on Saturday, ...?'
35. 'There isn't much coffee, ...?' 'No, but there is a lot of tea, ...?'
36. 'You mustn't do those things, ...?'
37. 'You can't all come to the party, ...?'
38. 'They didn't go to London on Sunday, ...?' 'No; they went on Monday, ...?'
39. 'You won't eat it all, ...?' 'No, but you will help me, ...?'
40. 'They haven't got a very big house, ...?' 'No, but they've got

Fill in the gaps 1

REPORTED QUESTIONS

1. 'Where do you live?' the man asked me.

....

2. 'What are you doing there?' I asked him.

....

3. 'Do you smoke?' he asked me.

....

4. 'Have you had breakfast?' he asked me.

....

5. 'Are you going to stay very long?' she asked him.

....

6. 'Do you want to go to the cinema?' Peter asked her.

....

7. 'Do you have any money on you?' they asked.

....

8. 'What time is it?' he demanded.

....

9. 'Are you living with your mother?' they asked her.

....

10. 'Do you have any relatives in this country?' they asked.

....

11. 'Where's the Central Bank?' 'asked the tourist.

....

12. 'How much is the ticket?' the Japanese demanded.

....

13. 'Why didn't you tell me?' she demanded.

....

14. 'What are you doing?' demanded the teacher.

....

15. 'What time is the train leaving?' the soldier asked.

....

16. 'How old is your mother?' they asked him.

....

17. 'Do you have a work permit?' he asked me.

....

18. 'What time did your brother come last night?' he asked me.

....

19. 'What time will you open next Saturday?' he asked.

....

20. 'Where are you from, little girl?' they asked.

....

REPORTED QUESTIONS

21. 'What have you been doing all afternoon?' they asked.

---

22. 'What are you doing tomorrow?' he asked her

---

23. 'Do you know anything about computers?' they asked me.

---

24. 'Do you know where you are?' they asked him.

---

25. 'What do you want?' the shop assistant asked.

---

26. 'Where can I buy video games?' he asked.

---

27. 'How much did the car cost you?' he asked me.

---

28. 'Did you hear anything last night?' the detective asked me.

---

29. 'Where can I change money?' the tourist asked.

---

30. 'Can I smoke in this compartment?' he asked.

---

31. 'Shall we meet again next year?' she asked.

---

32. 'Are you interested in working for us?' they asked.

---

33. 'What does this word mean?' the little girl asked.

---

34. 'How long have you been driving?' the policeman asked me.

---

35. 'Do they sell antiques in that shop?' he asked.

---

36. 'Where does your friend live?' asked my father.

---

37. 'Will you sell our house?' he demanded.

---

38. 'Have you thrown yesterday's paper away?' he asked her.

---

39. 'Could you speak Spanish when you were young?' she asked him.

---

40. 'Will you come with me if I ask you?' he asked her.
